It's
Christmas!

by Richard Sebra

BUMBA BOOKS™

LERNER PUBLICATIONS ◆ MINNEAPOLIS

Note to Educators:

Throughout this book, you'll find critical thinking questions. These can be used to engage young readers in thinking critically about the topic and in using the text and photos to do so.

Lerner Publications Company
A division of Lerner Publishing Group, Inc.
241 First Avenue North
Minneapolis, MN 55401 USA

For reading levels and more information, look up this title at www.lernerbooks.com.

Library of Congress Cataloging-in-Publication Data

Names: Sebra, Richard, 1984– author.
Title: It's Christmas / by Richard Sebra.
Description: Minneapolis : Lerner Publications, [2017] | Series: Bumba books—It's a Holiday! | Includes bibliographical references and index.
Identifiers: LCCN 2016001050 (print) | LCCN 2016011117 (ebook) | ISBN 9781512414264 (lb : alk. paper) | ISBN 9781512414950 (pb : alk. paper) | ISBN 9781512414967 (eb pdf)
Subjects: LCSH: Christmas—Juvenile literature.
Classification: LCC GT4985.5 .S43 2017 (print) | LCC GT4985.5 (ebook) | DDC 394.2663—dc23

LC record available at http://lccn.loc.gov/2016001050

Manufactured in the United States of America
1 – VP – 7/15/16

Expand learning beyond the printed book. Download free, complementary educational resources for this book from our website, www.lernerresource.com.

Table of Contents

Christmas Time

Christmas is a fun holiday.

People celebrate it around

the world.

It happens in winter.

It is on December 25.

Christmas is a Christian

holiday.

Many people go

to church.

People decorate their houses.

They hang lights.

They hang wreaths too.

How else might people decorate a house?

wreath

ornament

People put Christmas trees in their homes.

The trees are pretty.

They have many lights.

They have many ornaments.

Families get together.

They eat big meals.

Many families eat ham

or turkey.

Cookies are for dessert.

13

People give each other gifts.

The gifts are wrapped in paper.

Children often get toys.

What other gifts might children get?

People sing Christmas
songs.
Some people sing for
their neighbors.

Many people write Christmas cards.

They send the cards to friends.

They write about the past year.

What would you write in a Christmas card?

Christmas is a time of joy.

It is a time of celebration.

Christmas Calendar

Some people use special calendars to count down the days to Christmas.

Picture Glossary

church

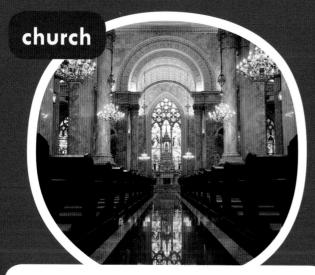

a place where people pray

gifts

items people give to each other on a holiday

ornaments

pretty things added to a Christmas tree

wreaths

circles of leaves or flowers

23

Index

Read More

Felix, Rebecca. *We Celebrate Christmas in Winter*. Ann Arbor, MI: Cherry Lake Publishing, 2014.

Pettiford, Rebecca. *Christmas*. Minneapolis: Jump!, 2015.

Stevens, Kathryn. *Christmas Trees*. Mankato, MN: The Child's World, 2015.

Photo Credits

The images in this book are used with the permission of: © Torwai Seubsri/Shutterstock.com, p. 5; © a454/Shutterstock.com, pp. 6–7, 23 (top left); © quackersnaps/iStock.com, pp. 9, 23 (bottom right); © EarnestTse/iStock.com, pp. 10, 23 (bottom left); © Monkey Business Images/Shutterstock.com, pp. 12–13, 18; © oliveromg/Shutterstock.com, pp. 14, 23 (top right); © Juanmonino/iStock.com, pp. 16–17; © monkeybusinessimages/iStock.com, p. 21; © evemilla/iStock.com, p. 22.

Front Cover: © RoJo.com/Shutterstock.com.